Designed For Success

Sports Cars

Revised & Updated

Heinemann
LIBRARY

Ian Graham

www.heinemann.co.uk/library
Visit our website to find out more information about **Heinemann Library** books.

To order:
 Phone 44 (0) 1865 888066
 Send a fax to 44 (0) 1865 314091
 Visit the Heinemann Bookshop at www.heinemann.co.uk/library to browse our catalogue and order online.

First published in Great Britain by Heinemann Library, Halley Court, Jordan Hill, Oxford, OX2 8EJ, part of Harcourt Education. Heinemann is a registered trademark of Harcourt Education Ltd.

Editorial: Andrew Farrow and Dan Nunn
Design: Steven Mead and Geoff Ward
Illustrations: Geoff Ward and Jeff Edwards
Picture Research: Melissa Allison
Production: Alison Parsons

Originated by Modern Age
Printed and bound in China by South China
    Printing Company

ISBN 978 0 431 16582 0 (hardback)
13 12 11 10 09 08
10 9 8 7 6 5 4 3 2 1

ISBN 978 0 431 16590 5 (paperback)
13 12 11 10 09 08
10 9 8 7 6 5 4 3 2 1

British Library Cataloguing-in-Publication Data
Graham, Ian, 1953 –
    Sports cars. – (Designed for success) 2nd edition
    1. Sports cars –- Juvenile literature
    I. Title
    629.2'221
A full catalogue record for this book is available from the British Library.

Acknowledgements
The publishers would like to thank the following for permission to reproduce photographs:
© Alvey and Towers pp. **21** (top), **28**; © ARIEL MOTOR COMPANY p. **27** (bottom); © Auto Express pp. **7**b-d, **16**, **18**, **25** (bottom), **27** (top), **26**, **29**; © Auto Express/Kenny P pp. **4**, **23** (top); © Auto Express/Phil Talbot p. **5** (top); © Bugatti Automobiles S.A.S pp. **10**, **11** (top), **14** (bottom), **15** (bottom); © Car Photo Library/David Kimber pp. **6**, **20** (bottom), **22**, **25** (top); © Corbis pp. **24** (bottom), **9** (top), **24** (top); © Corbis/Car Culture pp. **5**, **15** (top); © Corbis/Ted Soqul p. **13** (top); © Eye Ubiquitous p. **24** (bottom); © Eye Ubiquitous/Darren Maybury pp. **8**, **9** (bottom); © Getty Images/Ralph Orlowski p. **13** (bottom); © Kimball Stock/ Ron Kimball pp. **19**, **21**; © Lotus p. **7** (top); © Photoshot p. **11** (bottom); © SSC Autos p. **23** (bottom).

Background images by © istockphoto/Oliver Ritter-Wolff and © istockphoto/John Sfondilias.

Cover photograph reproduced with permission of Car Photo Library.

▷ Contents

Any words appearing in the text in bold, **like this**, are explained in the Glossary.

Sports cars

A car's design reflects the way it will be used. Some cars are designed to carry a whole family and their luggage. Others are designed for making short trips in busy city streets. Sports cars are high-**performance** cars that are designed to be fun to drive.

Most sports cars are designed as high-performance road cars. A few of them are more like racing cars that have been redesigned for use on public roads. The most powerful sports cars are often called "muscle cars". The most expensive are called supercars. Supercars are so expensive because they use the best materials and technology. There are no sharp divisions between these different types of high-performance cars. A powerful supercar might also be a muscle car.

Super car ▽

The Ferrari 599 GTB Fiorano is one of the fastest, most powerful, and most expensive cars in the world. It is almost a racing car for the road. Its engine was developed from a **Formula 1** racing-car engine. Inside, it is quite bare, just like a racing car. The 599 GTB Fiorano is a very high-performance sports car for super-rich drivers.

Cobra power ▷

One of the most famous sports cars was produced when an American ex-racing driver, Carroll Shelby, redesigned a British sports car, the AC Ace, and created the AC Cobra. It was a great road car and was also successful in motor racing. Its 4.7-litre **V8** engine gave it a top speed of up to 225 kph (140 mph). Later versions had larger engines, up to 7 litres, giving them a top speed of 265 kph (165 mph). The Cobra was so successful that **replicas** of them can still be bought in kit form for people to build for themselves.

BMW Z4 3.0SI SPORT

Engine size: 3.0-litre inline 6

Engine power: 265 hp

Length: 4.09 metres

Weight: 1,365 kg

Top speed: 250 kph (155 mph)

Seats: 2

Fun on wheels ▽

The German BMW Z4 is a typical modern sports car. It's a great-looking, open-top two-seater. It can be powered by a range of different engines to suit the performance that different drivers want.

Design for sport

A sports car's size, shape, weight, and engine power are chosen by its designer to give the car the nimble **performance** that sports cars are known for.

The size and shape of a sports car are very important. A small, lightweight car is more **manoeuvrable** than a big, heavy car. So, most sports cars are small and lightly built. There is often enough room inside for only a driver and one passenger. A sports car also has to be the right shape to slip through the air quickly. That is why most sports cars have a low-slung body sitting close to the ground. It has to look sporty and exciting, too. A smooth, gently curving body looks good and also lets air slide easily over the car. In many ways, the car's shape and design is decided by the performance it has to deliver.

Best-seller ▽

The Mazda MX-5 Miata is the world's best-selling sports car. It has the layout of a classic sports car. It is a small, open-top two-seater. It has an engine mounted at the front of the car, driving the rear wheels. All sports cars used to be built like this, because it is a good way to achieve the performance and **handling** necessary for a sports car.

Driving a lightweight ▷

The Lotus Elise can out-perform many sports cars with bigger and more powerful engines. The key to its success is its ultra-light weight. Its **chassis**, or frame, is made from **aluminium**, and its body is made from a material called **GRP** (Glass Reinforced Plastic). The whole car weighs only 860 kilograms. That's about half the weight of many high-performance cars. Its extreme lightness means that it can obtain racing-car performance from a smaller engine. The Elise is powered by a 1.8-litre, 134-**horsepower** engine.

◁ Open to the air

Even more fun than a sports car is an open-top sports car. Some sports cars have a fixed metal roof that can't be taken off. They're called fixed-head cars. Some have a detachable solid roof. Others have a roof made from soft material that folds away behind the seats. The Mercedes-Benz SLK is different. It has a solid roof that can fold like a soft roof at the flick of a switch. Within 30 seconds, the boot opens, the roof and rear window fold back out of sight, and the boot closes again.

MERCEDES-BENZ SLK 55 AMG

Engine size: 5.5-litre V8

Engine power: 360 hp

Length: 4.1 metres

Weight: 1,540 kg

Top speed: 250 kph (155 mph)

Seats: 2

▷ Track cars

The designers who create racing sports cars use every trick of technology and materials available to produce the fastest cars.

They often make use of parts and materials developed for other vehicles. For example, the **disc brakes** that slow racing cars down were originally developed for aircraft. Eventually, new technology that proves its worth on the racetrack is built into new road-going sports cars. Racing sports cars are light, powerful, and **streamlined**, just as road cars are. However, racing sports cars are even lighter, even more powerful, and even more streamlined than road-going sports cars. Racing sports cars also need to be stronger than road-going cars, to stand up to super-fast cornering without bending or twisting. To save weight, some of the parts that are usually made from steel are replaced by parts made from lighter materials. **Aluminium** and **carbon fibre** are often chosen.

Day and night at the ▽ wheel

Most motor races last up to about three hours, but the world-famous Le Mans sports car race lasts for 24 hours. Each of the specially designed cars is driven by a team of drivers who each take turns at the wheel. The fastest Le Mans sports cars can reach 350 kph (220 mph) on the fastest parts of the French racing circuit.

AUDI R10 LE MANS RACING CAR

Engine size: 5.5-litre V12 diesel

Engine power: 650 hp

Length: 4.65 metres

Weight: 925 kg

Top speed: 325 kph (200 mph)

Seats: 1

Cars with wings ▷

Racing sports cars often have a wing at the back. It works in the opposite way to an aircraft wing. As it cuts through the air, it pushes the car downwards. The faster the car goes, the more of this "**downforce**" the wing produces, pushing the car down more and more. This lets the car go round bends faster, because the tyres grip the track better.

rear wing

front wing

Speedy repairs ▷

Racing sports cars are designed to be taken apart very quickly. They may need to have damaged parts replaced. The nose and tail of the cars are usually detachable so that new ones can be fitted in a few seconds. During a long race, a car will probably also have its tyres replaced at least once. This is done by changing all the car's wheels, not just the tyres. A road car's wheels are each held in place by four or five nuts and bolts. A racing sports car's wheels are usually held on by one big nut. It can be spun off using a power tool and the wheel pulled off and replaced within a couple of seconds.

This Porsche 911 GT1-98 is having its wheels changed during a pit stop.

Bugatti Veyron

SUPER DESIGN

In the late 1990s, Bugatti and its parent company, Volkswagen, set out to build the ultimate high-**performance** car. The result was the Bugatti Veyron, one of the world's fastest and most powerful **production cars**.

A super-fast car needs a super-powerful engine. The Veyron is powered by a 1,001-**horsepower** engine made specially for it. It is the most powerful engine in any production car – more powerful even than NASCAR, Indy Car, and **Formula 1** racing car engines. For a car that can accelerate faster than a racing car and reach a top speed of more than 400 kph (250 mph), its shape is very important. The wrong shape could slow the car down, or make it dangerously unstable at high speeds. The Veyron's body is designed to let air flow around it as smoothly as possible. Every detail of the car is designed to be the best possible shape, weight, and strength.

Powerplant

The Bugatti Veyron's engine is unique. It is an 8-litre W16. The 16-**cylinder** W16 engine is made by combining two **V8** engines. An 8-litre engine normally produces about 500 horsepower. The Veyron's engine is twice as powerful as this because it is turbocharged – extra air is forced into it so that it can burn more **fuel** and produce more power.

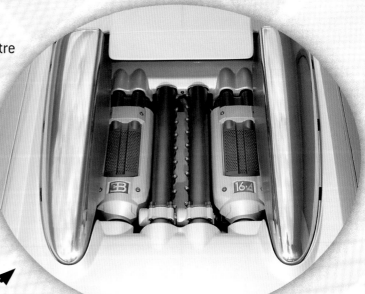

The Bugatti Veyron engine (pictured right) is controlled by a computer to ensure that it always works at peak performance.

Downforce

When the Veyron goes faster than 220 kph (137 mph), a wing is raised at the back. It works like an upside-down aircraft wing. Instead of lifting the car upwards, it pushes the car down. This presses the tyres harder against the ground and gives them more grip, helping to keep the car steady at high speeds. If the driver brakes, the wing tips up and works as an air-brake. Air hitting it slows the car down. It can stop it from 400 kph (250 mph) in less than 10 seconds.

Tunnel tests

Bugatti's engineers fine-tuned the car's shape by testing it in a **wind tunnel**. Wind tunnels are normally used for testing the shapes of airliners, fighter jets, and racing cars. The car was held still in the tunnel while air was blown through the tunnel. Hundreds of measurements of forces and **air pressures** all over the car were taken. Analysing these showed how well the car would perform and how steady it would be at all speeds. Wind tunnel tests enabled the car's designers to perfect its shape.

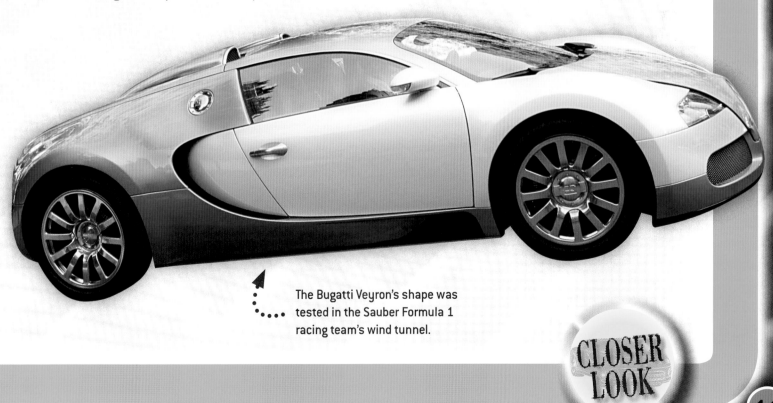

The Bugatti Veyron's shape was tested in the Sauber Formula 1 racing team's wind tunnel.

CLOSER LOOK

Bugatti Veyron
CARBON CONSTRUCTION

Road-going sports cars usually have a body made of steel, because steel can be cut, shaped, and welded quite easily. Steel is also readily available. However, there are other materials that are lighter and stronger than steel.

A few sports cars have an ultra-lightweight body made of glass reinforced plastic (**GRP**). More extreme high-**performance** cars like the Bugatti Veyron are made of **carbon fibre**. Carbon fibre is not used to build ordinary cars, because it is more expensive than steel and parts take longer to make from it. Carbon fibre parts have to be baked in an oven to harden them. Until the 1960s, most cars were built by making a strong frame and then covering it with thin sheets of steel. Cars are built quite differently today. The body provides a lot of the car's strength, so a separate frame is not needed. Doing away with the frame saves weight.

Structure

The driver and passenger sit inside a super-strong, but very lightweight, cell made of carbon fibre. The rest of the car, made mainly from **aluminium** and carbon fibre, is attached to the cell. In a crash, the front and back of the car are designed to soak up the impact by crumpling, protecting the people inside.

Carbon fibre survival cell

Aluminium rear section

Aluminium front section

Aluminium doors

Steel frame (carries engine)

Wheel deals

Even the Veyron's tyres are specially made for it. Ordinary tyres are not designed for the high speeds that the Veyron can reach. If a normal tyre were to burst at high speed, the car would swerve violently out of control. The Veyron's tyres are designed to keep running safely even if they suffer a puncture. The air pressures inside all four tyres are measured. If the pressure in any tyre falls, the driver is warned.

Air supply

At top speed, the Veyron's engine needs to take in 45,000 litres of air every minute. Even more air is needed to keep the engine and brakes cool. Two pipes, called snorkels, collect some of the air streaming over the car's roof and bring it down into the engine. Openings, called vents and scoops, in the car's body channel air through it to carry away unwanted heat.

CLOSER LOOK

Bugatti Veyron

MEGA CAR

The Bugatti Veyron can out-perform every other car on the road. Its combination of **acceleration**, speed, and **road-holding** are unmatched even by some racing cars.

From a standing start, the Veyron can reach 100 kph (60 mph) in only 2.5 seconds. Most sports cars take at least twice as long to reach the same speed. The BMX Z4 sports car takes nearly six seconds. Less than five seconds later, the Veyron reaches 200 kph (125 mph). This is about as fast as many family cars and sports cars can go, but it is only half-speed for the Veyron. If the driver carries on accelerating, the car tops 400 kph (250 mph) 55 seconds after it started. At this speed, it covers the length of a football pitch every second. It burns **fuel** so fast at top speed that its 100-litre fuel tank would be drained in less than 20 minutes.

Four wheel drive

A sports car's engine normally drives its rear wheels. The Veyron's engine produces far more power than two wheels could handle. Its engine powers all four wheels. The wheels are monitored by computer. If any of them begin to lose grip, the computer stops it from spinning wildly.

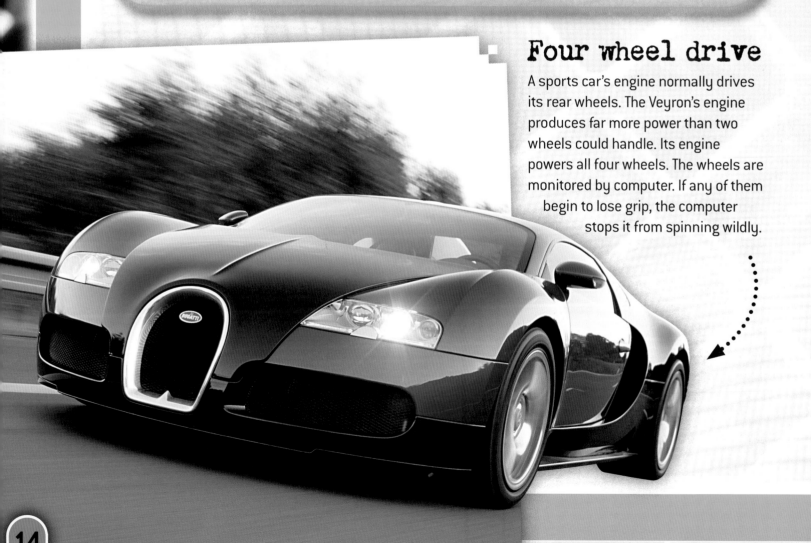

The inside story

Some of the world's fastest sports cars are modified racing cars, which are not designed for great comfort. The Bugatti Veyron is different. It is very luxurious indeed. Most of the interior is covered with the finest leather. The standard equipment includes air conditioning, a great stereo system, and satellite navigation. A PDA (Personal Digital Assistant) is supplied too. It is used to programme the navigation system and it can also download information from the car's computer.

BUGATTI VEYRON

Engine size: 8.0-litre W16

Engine power: 1,001 hp

Length: 4.46 metres

Weight: 1,888 kg

Top speed: 400 kph (250 mph)

Seats: 2

Ride height

The height of the Veyron's body above the ground depends on its speed. Up to 220 kph (136 mph), the car sits 125 mm (12.5 cm) above the ground. At higher speeds, it lowers itself to 80 mm (8 cm) at the front and higher at the back. To go faster than 375 kph (233 mph), the driver must stop the car and turn a key to select top speed mode. The car lowers itself to only 65 mm (6.5 cm) above the ground at the front.

CLOSER LOOK

Engine power

Sports cars are powered by the same sort of engines as most family cars. All engines are designed to release energy from **fuel** and use it to turn the car's wheels. However, sports car engines generally have higher **performance**.

Sports car engines have between four and twelve **cylinders**. Each cylinder is a tube with a close-fitting **piston** that slides up and down inside it. Fuel is sprayed into each cylinder in turn, squashed by the piston and **ignited** by an electric spark. The burning fuel produces hot gases that expand and push the piston back down the cylinder. The up-and-down movements of all the pistons are changed into a spinning motion that drives the car's wheels. Bigger cylinders hold more fuel and air, so a bigger engine is usually more powerful than a small engine. But bigger engines are also heavier. To keep a sports car light, its designers generally fit it with a small engine. However, the engine can't be too small or it will lack the necessary power. The designer has to balance power against weight to get the required performance.

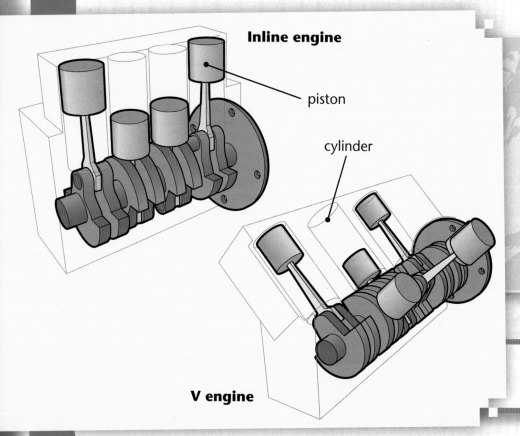

Inline engine

piston

cylinder

V engine

◁ Lines and Vs

The cylinders of an inline engine stand upright in a row. If a sports car designer wants to use a big engine with more than about six cylinders, there is not enough room to fit them in one long row. One answer is to have two rows, side by side, in the shape of a V. The **V8** (with eight cylinders) is a popular sports car engine.

Most sports cars are powered by an inline engine or a V8 engine.

Flat engines ▷

A few sports cars are powered by a third type of engine, called a flat engine or horizontally opposed engine. Its cylinders neither stand upright nor do they make a V shape. They lie flat, like bottles lying on their side. Flat engines are also known as boxer engines, because the pistons travel towards and away from each other like a boxer punching his fists together. The Porsche Boxster sports car is powered by a six-cylinder boxer engine, also called a flat 6.

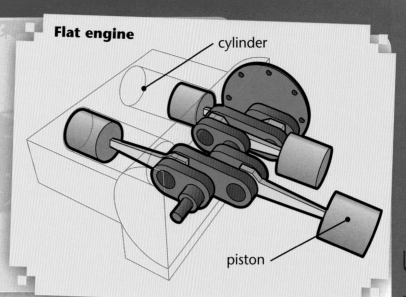

Flat engine

cylinder

piston

This illustration shows the combination of toothed wheels and shafts used to produce first and fourth gears.

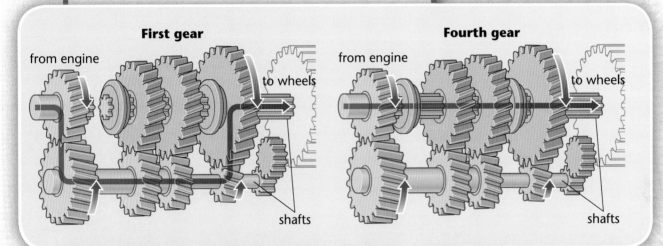

First gear

from engine

to wheels

shafts

Fourth gear

from engine

to wheels

shafts

A box of teeth! △

A sports car engine turns a set of toothed wheels in the **gearbox**. The gearbox is connected, through **shafts**, to the car's wheels. The driver chooses which **gear** to use. By changing gear, the driver can make the engine drive the car's wheels at anything from walking pace to its top speed.

PORSCHE BOXSTER S

Engine size: 3.4-litre flat 6

Engine power: 295 hp

Length: 4.4 metres

Weight: 1,355 kg

Top speed: 270 kph (169 mph)

Seats: 2

Muscle cars

Some high-**performance** cars owe their **acceleration** and speed to an enormous engine under the bonnet.

The smallest city cars have an engine less than 1 litre in size. That's smaller than some motorcycle engines! An engine this size produces as little as 50 **horsepower**. A small sports car is driven by an engine roughly twice this size and power. A **Formula 1** racing car is powered by a 2.4-litre engine. But this is small compared to muscle cars. They are powered by engines of 5 litres or more – sometimes a lot more! These big-engine chargers include the USA's Chevrolet Corvette and Ford Mustang, but the classic muscle car is the Dodge Viper. Its driver sits behind a massive 8.4-litre, 600-horsepower engine. No wonder the car has such a long bonnet!

America's △ wild horse

The US Ford Mustang is the most famous car in the USA and also the USA's best-selling muscle car. It was designed in the early 1960s to appeal to a new generation of young motorists looking for a more exciting drive. Since then, it has been redesigned and updated year after year. Today, with a 4.6-litre **V8** engine growling in front of the driver, the Mustang can reach 100 kph (60 mph) in about 5 seconds and reach a top speed of about 240 kph (150 mph).

The Dodge Viper SRT-10 is one of the most powerful muscle cars.

Highway snake △

The Dodge Viper started life as a "concept car". Concept cars show what designers think future cars might look like. Many of them are never manufactured, but so many people liked the Viper concept that Dodge decided to build it. Its huge engine was developed from a truck engine. Its body was carefully designed to look good and also to remain stable at high speeds.

DODGE VIPER SRT-10

Engine size: 8.4-litre V10

Engine power: 600 hp

Length: 4.5 metres

Weight: 1,560 kg

Top speed: 320 kph (200 mph)

Seats: 2

The original Chevrolet Corvette (pictured here) was the first US sports car. It went on sale in 1953.

A US favourite ▽

Since the first Corvette went on sale more than 50 years ago, it has been updated regularly. In that time, the engine has grown in size from 3.9 litres to 6.0 litres, and it has also nearly trebled in power from 150 horsepower to 400 horsepower.

Smooth bodies

The shape of a sports car affects its **acceleration**, top speed, and **handling**. Designing the right shape improves its **performance**.

When a sports car moves, it has to push the air out of the way. Some of the engine's power is wasted in overcoming this air resistance, or **drag**. Different shapes cause different amounts of drag. A smooth body is better, because no parts stick out to catch the air rushing past the car. Some sports cars have their engine behind the driver. This lets the designer lower the front of the car and so reduce the drag it produces. However, designing a sports car is as much about making the car fun to drive as it is about producing a perfect design. A traditional sports car has an engine at the front and an open top. This isn't the fastest shape, but it's great fun to drive.

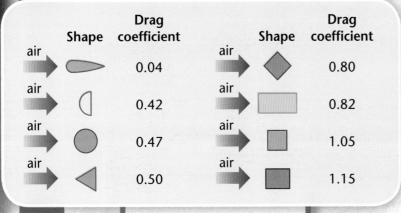

	Shape	Drag coefficient		Shape	Drag coefficient
air		0.04	air		0.80
air		0.42	air		0.82
air		0.47	air		1.05
air		0.50	air		1.15

This diagram shows the different coefficient of drag numbers produced by a selection of different shapes. The shapes with the smallest number give the least drag.

It's such a drag! ▽

The most **streamlined** sports cars are designed to create the least air resistance, or drag. The shape of the car is tested to find out how easily it slips through the air. The tests produce a number, called the "coefficient of drag", which shows how "slippery" the car is. The smaller the number, the more slippery it is. For a car the shape of a brick, the number is 1.0 or more. For a boxy family car, it is about 0.38. For very streamlined cars, like the Ferrari Enzo (pictured below), it is 0.30 or less.

Cool bodies ▷

Designing a car's body is made more complicated because it has to have holes in it. If the body was completely closed, the engine would be starved of air, and would overheat and break down. The engine needs air to burn its **fuel** and for cooling. The air enters the body through holes called ducts. They are carefully designed to let in the right amount of air without causing lots of drag.

A Ferrari Testarossa with air intake ducts on the sides.

So smooth ▽

The Porsche Cayman S has a very streamlined body. Its headlights sit beneath streamlined glass covers. Its wing mirrors are beautifully curved too, so that air slips around them easily. Its windows wrap around the car in line with the body. There are no bumps in the bodywork that might slow down the air flowing around the car.

PORSCHE CAYMAN S

Engine size: 3.4-litre flat 6

Engine power: 295 hp

Length: 4.4 metres

Weight: 1,340 kg

Top speed: 275 kph (170 mph)

Seats: 2

The lines in this picture show how air flows around the smoothly curving shape of a streamlined car.

Supercars

Supercars are the fastest and most expensive high-**performance** sports cars. They are capable of racing-car performance on the road, but only the wealthiest motorists can afford to buy a supercar.

Sports cars are small, lightweight cars, but supercars are often bigger and heavier. Extra weight slows a car down, but supercars more than make up for their weight in two ways. First, they have much more powerful engines than other sports cars. More power produces faster **acceleration**. Most supercars can accelerate from zero to 100 kph (60 mph) in less than four seconds. Second, they have a very **streamlined** shape to reduce **drag**, or air resistance. The combination of high power and streamlined shape gives supercars very high top speeds. Most supercars can go faster than 320 kph (200 mph)!

Lamborghini Murciélago ▽

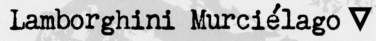

The Lamborghini Murciélago is a remarkable machine. Inside its elegant, swooping body, a huge, roaring 6.5-litre engine sits behind the driver. The 640-**horsepower** engine can accelerate the 1.6-tonne car to about 340 kph (210 mph). Acceleration is helped by the fact that most of the body parts, apart from the roof and the doors, are made from lightweight **carbon fibre**.

LAMBORGHINI MURCIÉLAGO LP640

Engine size: 6.5-litre V12

Engine power: 640 hp

Length: 4.6 metres

Weight: 1,665 kg

Top speed: 340 kph (210 mph)

Seats: 2

Koenigsegg CCX ▷

The CCX is the latest supercar from the Swedish car-maker, Koenigsegg. In 2005, the car that came before it, the CCR, set a world-record speed for **production cars** of 388 kph (240 mph). Like the CCR, the new CCX is formed from carbon fibre for maximum lightness, strength, and speed. This car is equally at home on the race-track and public roads. For open-top driving in good weather, its roof can be taken off and stowed under the front bonnet.

The ultimate supercar ▽

The Ultimate Aero TT is a supercar built by SSC (Shelby Super Cars) in the USA. The car is the result of seven years of work by the company's design team. Tests in a NASA (the US space agency) **wind tunnel** showed that the car may be able to reach a top speed of 440 kph (273 mph) in the right conditions.

▷ Designing for safety

Modern sports cars are designed to be safe. If the worst happens and a sports car is involved in an accident, it is designed to protect the people inside it.

When a car hits something, it stops incredibly suddenly. Our soft bodies are easily damaged by the violent forces in a collision. Some of a sports car's safety features are designed to let the occupants come to a halt a little less suddenly. The seats, doors, and **dashboard** are padded. Seatbelts hold the occupants safely in their seats and stop them from being hurled out through the windscreen. However, a seatbelt does not hold the head. It can fly forwards, causing neck injuries, and the driver's head may hit the steering wheel. To prevent this, cars are now often fitted with airbags that inflate and cushion the head in the event of an accident.

Belt up! △

Seatbelts normally allow a driver or passenger to move around freely. But when a car hits something, the belt locks and stops the person wearing it from travelling forwards. Some sports cars are fitted with an extra safety feature called a pre-tensioner. In a collision, the seatbelt doesn't just lock, it actually tightens and pulls the driver or passenger back into the seat.

◁ Safety bags

When a car hits something, **sensors** detect the sudden stop and trigger the airbags. An **igniter** sets off a gas capsule that blows up the bag like a balloon. All of this happens within a fraction of a second. It has to be that quick to catch the driver's head before it hits the steering wheel.

Rock and roll ▷

Convertible or open-top sports cars often have a thick bar that loops up behind the seats, above the driver's head. This is a roll bar and it has a life-saving purpose. If the car turns over, it supports the weight of the car and stops it from crushing the occupants underneath. Some cars that seem to have no roll bar have a very strong windscreen frame that does the same job.

The Ferarri 360 Spider has an individual roll bar for each seat.

Crash test dummies ▽

All new car designs are tested by deliberately crashing them to make sure that they meet international safety regulations. Inside the car are life-size dummies designed to resemble a human driver and passengers. They weigh the same as people and they have joints in all the right places. They are also fitted with instruments to record the forces that act on them during a crash.

Fun cars

A handful of sports cars are designed to be totally impractical for anything but having fun. They're designed and built for drivers to enjoy driving. Most of them look very basic indeed. They seem little more than an engine, a seat, and four wheels. Because they are so basic, they are also amazingly light.

The tiny Caterham 7 Superlight R400, for example, is as powerful as a 4-litre Ford Mustang. However, the Caterham is less than one third of the Mustang's weight. This combination of more power and less weight produces eye-poppingly fast **acceleration**, sharper turning, and higher speeds. The Superlight R400 can get from zero to 100 kph (60 mph) in 3.8 seconds, compared to 7.8 seconds for the Mustang.

Caterham 7 ▽

The Caterham 7 has been produced in one form or another since it was launched as the Lotus 7 in 1957. It's an open-topped, ultra-lightweight car. There are several different engines. The model below was a special edition produced in 2001. The cars weigh about 500 kg. That's less than one third of the weight of a Ford Mustang.

CATERHAM 7 SUPERLIGHT R400

Engine size: 2.0-litre inline 4

Engine power: 210 hp

Length: 3.1 metres

Weight: 500 kg

Top speed: 225 kph (140 mph)

Seats: 2

On the prowl ▷

The Plymouth Prowler is designed to look dramatic and turn heads in the street. Its styling was inspired by cars called hot rods, built by car enthusiasts in the USA. Some hot rods are built for racing. Others are built for show. They're often built to look like old-fashioned family cars, but under their outer bodies they have a very powerful engine. The interior is often luxurious, with leather seats and a super sound system. The fun shape and extra weight of the hi-fi, luxurious interior, and other additions affect the car's **performance**.

The designer of the Plymouth Prowler had to balance appearance and "street-cred" against performance, **handling**, and speed.

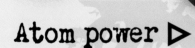

Atom power ▷

The British Ariel Atom looks like a metal skeleton on wheels. It has no doors, no windscreen, and no roof. There is nowhere to store luggage. It certainly isn't **streamlined** either. And yet it is very fast – its top speed is 225 kph (140 mph). Its secret is that it is a whopping 404 kilograms lighter than the ultra-light Lotus Elise sports car, and has 86 more **horsepower** than the Elise.

Every sports car is designed with a particular type of driver in mind. This table compares the basic specifications of some of today's best-known sports cars.

Car	Engine	Weight (kilograms)	Top speed (kph / mph)	Time (seconds) 0–100 kph (0–60 mph)
Ariel Atom 190	2.0-litre inline 4	456	225 / 140	2.9
Audi R10 Le Mans car	5.5-litre V12 diesel	925	325 / 200	unknown
BMW Z4 3.0si Sport	3.0-litre inline 6	1,365	250 / 155	5.9
Bugatti Veyron	8.0-litre W16	1,888	400 / 250	2.5
Caterham 7 Superlight R400	2.0-litre inline 4	500	225 / 140	3.8
Chevrolet Corvette Coupe	6.0-litre V8	1,458	300 / 185	4.2
Dodge Viper SRT10	8.4-litre V10	1,560	320 / 200	3.8
Ferrari 599 GTB Fiorano	6.0-litre V12	1,690	330 / 205	3.7
Ferrari F50	4.7-litre V12	1,350	325 / 202	3.7
Ford Mustang GT	4.6-litre V8	1,582	240 / 150	5.2
Koenigsegg CCX	4.7-litre V8	1,180	400 / 250	3.2
Lamborghini Murciélago LP640	6.5-litre V12	1,665	340 / 210	3.4
Lotus Elise S	1.8-litre inline 4	860	205 / 127	5.8
Mazda MX-5 Miata	2.0-litre inline 4	1,155	210 / 130	7.9
Mercedes-Benz SLK 55 AMG	5.5-litre V8	1,540	250 / 155	4.9
Porsche Boxster S	3.4-litre flat 6	1,355	270 / 169	5.4
Porsche Cayman S	3.4-litre flat 6	1,340	275 / 170	5.4
SSC Ultimate Aero TT	6.2-litre V8	1,245	440 / 273	2.8

Jaguar's E-type ▷

In the 1960s, one of the most famous sports cars in the world was the Jaguar E-type. Originally the E-type was designed as a racing car. However, when Jaguar pulled out of motor racing, the E-type was redesigned as a road car. A 1961 model with a 3.8-litre engine could reach 240 kph (150 mph).

Books and magazines

Daily Express World Car Guide, Daily Express
The Haynes Car Guide (J. H. Haynes, 2008)
The World's Fastest Cars, Michael Martin (Capstone Press, 2006)
Ultimate Cars, Matt Saunders (J. H. Haynes, 2006)
Sports Cars: 2 (Mean Machines), Chris Oxlade (Raintree Publishers, 2004)

Websites

http://auto.howstuffworks.com
A website with simple explanations for how engines and other parts of cars work.

http://www.beaulieu.co.uk/motormuseum/introduction.cfm
The website of the National Motor Museum in England.

http://www.carsofthestars.com
Cars driven by the stars, including some of the high-performance cars driven by James Bond.

http://www.sportscarcup.com
Details of dozens of sports cars.

http://www.2sportscars.com/sports-cars.shtml
Sports car pictures and specifications.

Ferrari's "Red Head" ▷

Sports cars became very popular in the 1950s. Ferrari built one of its famous sports cars, the Testarossa, in 1956. It was called Testarossa (Italian for "red head") after the red covers on top of the engine. It was a racing sports car and it was very successful indeed. Its 300-**horsepower**, 3-litre **V12** engine and lightweight **alloy** body gave it a top speed of about 270 kph (170 mph).

Glossary

acceleration go faster – a driver accelerates by pressing the accelerator pedal

air pressure pushing effect of air pressing against a surface

alloy metal made from a mixture of two or more different metals

aluminium lightweight metal that is easy to bend and shape

carbon fibre strong and lightweight material made from strands of carbon embedded in hard plastic

chassis frame on which a vehicle is built

cylinder a tube-shaped part of a car engine where the fuel is burned. A sports car may have between four and twelve cylinders.

dashboard another name for a car's instrument panel

disc brakes brakes made of a disc (attached to a vehicle's wheel) between two tough pads. The disc spins with the wheel. When the driver presses the brake pedal, the pads grip the disc and slow it down.

downforce a force that presses a car down onto the road. It can be produced by a wing or by the shape of the car itself. Downforce helps a car to corner faster without skidding, because its tyres grip the ground better.

drag resistance to a car's movement through the air, caused by the air itself. As a car moves forwards, it has to push the air out of the way and the air pushes back. Drag is also called air resistance.

Formula 1 leading international motor racing championship

fuel a substance that is burned to produce power. Sports cars' engines burn petrol, a liquid made from oil.

gear a wheel with teeth around its edge. When two gear wheels are put together so that their teeth interlock, turning one wheel makes the other wheel turn too. If the wheels are the same size, they turn at the same speed. If one wheel is much bigger or smaller than the other, the wheels turn at different speeds.

gearbox set of gear wheels of different sizes. By linking different gear wheels so that their teeth lock together, the engine can be made to turn the car's wheels at a much wider range of speeds. Selecting different gear wheels like this is also called "changing gear".

GRP (Glass Reinforced Plastic) a material often used in car construction. GRP is made from glass fibres embedded in plastic. It is easily moulded into the shape of a car's body. Some sports cars have a GRP body because GRP is lighter than metal.

handling way a car responds or reacts when it is being driven, and how well it holds the road

horsepower (hp) measurement showing how much work an engine can do

ignite set on fire – the fuel inside an engine is set on fire by an electric spark

manoeuvrable steerable. A more manoeuvrable car can make tighter turns than most other cars.

performance capabilities. A high-performance car is capable of faster acceleration and higher speeds than most cars.

piston the part of a car's engine that slides back and forth inside the cylinder where the fuel is burned. Each time the fuel is burned, the piston is pushed down the cylinder. The back and forth movements turn the car's wheels.

production car car built in large numbers for sale

replica precise copy. A replica car is a modern copy of an older model.

road-holding a car's ability to grip the road without skidding, especially as it turns corners

sensors devices that take measurements. Sensors measure everything from engine temperature to oil pressure. They are connected to the instruments in front of the driver and to the car's computer, if it has one.

shaft revolving rod. Shafts are used in cars to transmit motion or power from one place to another, from the engine to the wheels for example.

streamlined designed to move through air very easily, producing very little air resistance. Smooth, gently-curving shapes are more streamlined than rough or boxy shapes. A fish's body is one of the most streamlined shapes.

V8, V12 type of car engine with eight, or twelve, cylinders. The cylinders are arranged in two rows, or "banks". The two rows of cylinders spin a shaft that runs along the bottom of the engine. The cylinders lean outwards from this shaft, giving the engine its V shape. The number after the V shows how many cylinders the engine has.

wind tunnel large pipe that air is blown through, used for testing how cars and other vehicles behave at different speeds. Instead of being driven through the air, the car stays still and the air is blown at the car. Small models of cars are often used, but some wind tunnels are big enough for full-size cars.

Index

SPORTS CARS